Canadian Families
CANADIAN CELEBRATIONS

TRUE NORTH

BY TODD KORTEMEIER

True North is published by Beech Street Books
27 Stewart Rd. Collingwood, ON Canada L9Y 4M7

www.beechstreetbooks.ca

Produced by Red Line Editorial

Photographs ©: Monkey Business Images/iStockphoto, cover, 1; Sergei Bachlakov/Shutterstock Images, 4–5; Monkey Business Images/Shutterstock Images, 6; mikecphoto/Shutterstock Images, 8–9; Panitchon/Shutterstock Images, 10–11; Red Line Editorial, 12; David P. Lewis/Shutterstock Images, 14–15; meunierd/Shutterstock Images, 16; szefei/Shutterstock Images, 18–19; Ryerson Clark/iStockphoto, 20–21

Editor: Heather C. Hudak
Designer: Laura Polzin

Library and Archives Canada Cataloguing in Publication

Kortemeier, Todd, 1986-, author
    Canadian celebrations / by Todd Kortemeier.

(Canadian families)
Includes bibliographical references and index.
Issued in print and electronic formats.
ISBN 978-1-77308-006-2 (hardback).--ISBN 978-1-77308-034-5 (paperback).--
ISBN 978-1-77308-062-8 (pdf).--ISBN 978-1-77308-090-1 (html)

    1. Holidays--Canada--Juvenile literature. 2. Festivals--Canada--Juvenile
literature. I. Title.

GT4813.A2K67 2016   j394.26971   C2016-903549-2
                                               C2016-903550-6

Printed in the United States of America
Mankato, MN
August 2016

TABLE OF CONTENTS

WINTER WONDERS

Canada in winter can be a wonderland. It's full of fun things to do and reasons to celebrate. Canadians take part in many celebrations throughout the season.

One of the biggest winter celebrations is Christmas. **Cultures** celebrate Christmas differently around the world. They bring these **traditions** to Canada. In most cultures people give gifts to each other. They get together with family. They eat big meals and enjoy winter activities.

In Quebec, most people are French Canadian. On Christmas Eve, they have a big meal. It is called Réveillon. It lasts late into the night. People go to church

Chinese New Year is a 15-day festival. It begins on a different day each year.

FAST FACT

In Canada New Year's Day is January 1. But in China people use a different calendar. Their new year starts later. Big cities often have a neighbourhood called Chinatown. Many Chinese people live in these communities. Victoria, British Columbia, has the country's oldest Chinatown. There is a local Chinese New Year celebration. It features parades and traditional foods.

Canadian people come from many cultures. Even among those who celebrate Christmas, there are many different holiday traditions.

at midnight. Santa Claus is a beloved Christmas figure. In French he is called Père Nöel.

In Newfoundland and Labrador, there is a tradition called mummering. People go house-to-house spreading Christmas cheer. They dress up in costumes and sing Christmas songs.

Canadians who don't celebrate Christmas might take part in other December holidays. Jewish people celebrate **Hanukkah**. African-Canadian people celebrate **Kwanzaa**. These celebrations all feature fun and time with family.

Aboriginal Canadians have long celebrated the winter **solstice**. It takes place between December 21 and 23 each year. It is the shortest day and longest night of the year. After the solstice, days get longer. The warmer weather and longer days make it easier to hunt, travel, and do daily tasks. Northern communities, such as Whitehorse in Yukon, celebrate the solstice with music and dancing.

FAST FACT

First Nations in Canada have played games in the winter for hundreds of years. Those games turned into an official competition. It is also a celebration of winter fun. The Arctic Winter Games are held every two years. They're only played in Arctic communities, such as Yellowknife, in the Northwest Territories. Many Aboriginal Canadians take part, and other northern people do, too.

Chapter Two

SPRING EVENTS

Canadians hold many types of celebrations in spring. One holiday is Victoria Day. It honours Queen Victoria's birthday and the birthday of the current British **monarch**.

Victoria Day takes place on the Monday before May 24. This gives many Canadians a three-day weekend. They enjoy warm spring weather. People often take vacations or go camping. They may have barbecues and spend time with family. Most cities have fireworks shows. One spectacular display takes place over Niagara Falls in Ontario.

Many cities have fireworks on Victoria Day.

FAST FACT

Victoria Day celebrates the connection between Canada and the United Kingdom. The Canadian flag is flown alongside the British flag, the Union Jack. The red, white, and blue flag flies beside the Canadian maple leaf from sunrise to sunset that day.

Easter is a big holiday for Christians. It takes place in March or April each year. Families get together to share meals. Children hunt for hidden Easter eggs and enjoy chocolate bunnies and other sweet treats. Vegreville, Alberta, is home to the world's largest Easter egg. Made of metal, it is more than 9 metres tall. Good Friday happens two days before Easter Sunday. Almost everyone in Canada gets the day off from work or school.

Buddhists in Canada celebrate Vesak in May. It celebrates the birthday of Buddha. He founded their religion. Buddhists in Vancouver celebrated a citywide

FAST FACT

Quebec has National Patriots' Day. It is celebrated instead of Victoria Day. It honours the people who fought for Quebec's **independence** from the United Kingdom in the 1830s. It celebrates Quebec's unique history and culture through parades and reenactments of historical events.

Many people have statues of Buddha in their homes. Some may celebrate Vesak. Vesak is also known as Buddha Day.

HOLIDAYS THROUGHOUT THE YEAR

JANUARY

NEW YEAR'S DAY

FEBRUARY

ISLANDER DAY
(PRINCE EDWARD ISLAND)

LOUIS RIEL DAY
(MANITOBA)

FAMILY DAY
(BRITISH COLUMBIA, ALBERTA, SASKATCHEWAN, MANITOBA, ONTARIO)

MARCH

GOOD FRIDAY
(MAY FALL IN APRIL)

EASTER MONDAY
(MAY FALL IN APRIL)

APRIL

ST. GEORGE'S DAY
(NEWFOUNDLAND AND LABRADOR)

MAY

VICTORIA DAY

JUNE

NATIONAL ABORIGINAL DAY

SAINT-JEAN-BAPTISTE DAY
(QUEBEC)

DISCOVERY DAY
(NEWFOUNDLAND AND LABRADOR)

JULY

CANADA DAY

NUNAVUT DAY
(NUNAVUT)

AUGUST

CIVIC HOLIDAY
(AUGUST LONG WEEKEND)

SEPTEMBER

LABOUR DAY

OCTOBER

THANKSGIVING

NOVEMBER

REMEMBERANCE DAY

DECEMBER

CHRISTMAS DAY
BOXING DAY

Some holidays vary by province and territory.

12

festival in 2015 with prayer and chanting. It was the first celebration of its kind in Vancouver.

On the northwest coast of British Columbia, First Nations groups, such as the Heiltsuk and Haida, have held big feasts called potlatches for hundreds of years. In the past most potlatches were held for big events, such as weddings or births. Today, First Nations groups hold them as a link to the past. They are not as large as they used to be. Still, they feature huge feasts and celebrate big events.

Powwows are similar to potlatches. They were first held by Plains First Nations, such as the Blackfoot. Powwows are still held today. They include dancing and music.

INQUIRY QUESTIONS

What celebrations does your family have? What celebrations do your friends and classmates have? How are they different from your family's celebrations?

Chapter Three

SUMMER ACTIVITIES

Summer in Canada is a great time. The warm weather and break from school make for a lot of fun.

The biggest summer holiday is Canada Day. It is known as Canada's birthday. Canada became a country on July 1, 1867. Ever since, its birthday has been celebrated on the same day each year. The holiday has been known as Canada Day since 1983.

On Canada Day many people attend parades and watch fireworks. They invite friends and family over for barbecues. Many cities and towns hold celebrations. One of the biggest celebrations is in Canada's capital,

Some people wave Canadian flags and wear red on Canada Day.

Some people take part in parades on Saint-Jean-Baptiste Day.

Ottawa. There are dance and musical performances. Military planes fly overhead.

Canada Day is one of four holidays that are part of the Celebrate Canada festivities. Saint-Jean-Baptiste Day is also known as Quebec

National Day. It takes place on June 24 in Quebec. It honours the province's patron saint. National Aboriginal Day takes place on June 21. Canadian Multiculturalism Day happens on June 27. Both of these holidays celebrate the many cultures that live in Canada. Events take place all across the country.

Summer is the time for many festivals. A lot of these celebrate local foods. There's the Pictou Lobster Carnival in Pictou, Nova Scotia, in July. Altona, Manitoba, hosts the Sunflower Festival late in July. It celebrates the local **crops**. Sunflowers are the highlight.

The Adäka Cultural Festival also takes place in July. It is held in Whitehorse, Yukon. It is a weeklong celebration of the local First Nations culture. There are dances and musical performances. People make Aboriginal arts and **crafts**, such as birch baskets.

Chapter Four

FALL FUN

The weather starts to get cold in fall. But it is still a time of great celebration. Thanksgiving takes place on the second Monday in October. It is a type of **harvest** festival. People give thanks for food or for anything good in their lives.

Thanksgiving is all about food and family. Canadians travel across the country to be together. Turkey and pumpkin pie are common menu items.

On Halloween children dress up in costumes. They go door to door seeking candy. Some people throw costume parties. People carve designs in pumpkins.

Diwali takes place in October or November. It is the biggest Indian holiday. It celebrates the last harvest before winter. People light clay lamps.

FAST FACT

Remembrance Day takes place on November 11. It honours Canadians who have served or lost their lives in military service. People wear poppy flowers on their clothing as a reminder. At 11 a.m., Canadians stop what they are doing. They have a moment of silence to remember the lives lost.

Picking out a pumpkin to carve is a fun family activity.

Many people of German **heritage** live in the Kitchener-Waterloo area of Ontario. They hold Oktoberfest. It is one of Germany's biggest celebrations. The Kitchener-Waterloo Oktoberfest has been held each year since 1969. It is the largest Oktoberfest in the world outside Germany. Oktoberfest is a big party that anyone can take part in. People enjoy German foods, music, and dancing.

Jewish people celebrate Yom Kippur in the fall. They spend most of the day praying. There are Jewish people all over Canada. But Ontario has the largest **population**.

People pin poppies over their hearts on Remembrance Day.

GLOSSARY

CRAFTS
items handmade by a skilled person

CROPS
plants grown for food or other uses

CULTURES
sets of traits unique to a group of people

HANUKKAH
a Jewish holiday that is celebrated over eight days and nights in late November or December

HARVEST
the collection and gathering of crops

HERITAGE
the history of a people

INDEPENDENCE
the act of being free from outside control

KWANZAA
a holiday that takes place between December 26 and January 1 and celebrates African-Canadian peoples' culture and traditions

LEASES
agreements for the use of something

MONARCH
a king or queen

POPULATION
all of the people living in a certain place

SOLSTICE
the two times a year when the sun is farthest from or closest to Earth

TRADITIONS
sets of activities or beliefs repeated throughout history

TO LEARN MORE

BOOKS

Aloian, Molly. *Cultural Traditions in Canada*. New York: Crabtree Publishing, 2014.

Creasey, Eleanor. *On Remembrance Day*. Toronto: Dundurn Press, 2014.

Peppas, Lynn. *Victoria Day*. New York: Crabtree Publishing, 2012.

WEBSITES

THE CANADIAN ENCYCLOPEDIA: FESTIVALS
www.thecanadianencyclopedia.ca/en/article/festivals

GOVERNMENT OF CANADA: CALENDAR OF CULTURAL EVENTS
http://canada.pch.gc.ca/eng/1454353213978

GOVERNMENT OF CANADA: EVENTS, CELEBRATIONS AND COMMEMORATIONS
http://canada.pch.gc.ca/eng/1444411481693/1444411709508

INDEX

ABOUT THE AUTHOR

Todd Kortemeier is a journalist, an editor, and a children's book author. He has authored dozens of books for young people on a wide variety of topics.